The Wild Ponies
of Assateague Island

By Donna K. Grosvenor

Photographs by James L. Stanfield

■ BOOKS FOR YOUNG EXPLORERS
NATIONAL GEOGRAPHIC SOCIETY

There is a place where wild ponies live free to race the wind.
The place is an island called Assateague.
Assateague lies on the edge of the salty ocean.

On the island the ponies have plenty of grass for food.
There are pools of water for drinking
and shady pine trees for shelter.

A mother pony, called a mare, is going to have a baby.

After her baby is born, the mother licks and nuzzles it.

Baby ponies are called foals.

The mare welcomes her new foal by touching noses.

She sniffs to learn her baby's smell.

This helps the mother find her foal among the other ponies.

A foal struggles to stand up only a few minutes after she is born.

Her legs are still wobbly, but she is strong and healthy.

In a few hours she will run, and play, and discover the world around her.

New foals are very hungry. Their first discovery
is mother's nipples, and the foals suck the warm, sweet milk.
The mother's milk is all the food the new foal needs.
Later, there is also time for fun.
One foal bites a piece of paper and plays a lively game.

At first the foals follow their mothers like little shadows.

But soon the young ponies make friends with each other.

Ponies say hello by rubbing noses and by nibbling muzzles or ears.

Foals like to play by jumping and rearing on their hind legs.

These games help the ponies grow strong.

When the ponies are sleepy, they close their eyes and yawn.

On a lazy, warm day the foals stretch out to soak up the sunshine.

Other ponies stand beneath the shady pine trees or graze on tender, salty grass.

The ponies live in families called herds.

In each herd there are several mares and a strong male pony. He is called a stallion.

The stallion is the leader of the herd. It is his job to protect his mares and foals.

Can you find the black-and-white stallion? He stands alone watching over his herd.

Stallions must be like watchmen. They are always on guard.

Any strange sight or sound can mean danger.

At the first sign of danger, the stallion warns his mares and foals.

The mares know the stallion's danger signal.

He pulls his ears back and he stretches his neck down low to the ground.

Then he moves his head from side to side, as if he were dancing to music.

This signal sends his herd running off at a gallop.

If a mare doesn't move fast enough, the stallion might nip her with his teeth.

The stallion follows behind. He is ready to turn and protect his herd.

Stallions try to steal mares from each other.
So when two stallions meet, they often fight.
But first they may stand head to head and stare at each other.
Then each stallion tries to show he is stronger.
The stallions throw their heads back and toss their tails.
They paw the ground and make loud snorting noises.
Showing off this way gives one stallion time
to change his mind and leave before a fight begins.

One stallion splashes after another into the water and bites him on the back.

When stallions fight,
they bite and kick.
Young stallions learn to fight
by playing fighting games.
When wild stallions grow up,
the strongest and smartest
learn to steal mares
and start herds of their own.

17

Assateague seems far from the noisy world.
A fox moves through the woods
with barely a sound.
The fox carries a duck dinner in its mouth.
A deer stands as quietly as a shadow.
Only the calls of the water birds
break the silence.
Assateague belongs to the wild creatures.

Life on Assateague can be hard.
Ocean storms cover the island with thick fog.
During a stinging rain, a foal uses his mother's neck
for an umbrella. The heavy rains make deep mudholes
that can trap the ponies.
Winter brings biting cold.
Summer brings flies and so many mosquitoes
that they look like dark clouds.
But somehow strong little ponies have lived
on the island for hundreds of years.

Once a year there is a pony roundup, called Pony Penning.

Every July, people from nearby Chincoteague Island come to Assateague.

Men on horseback ride through the tall grass and bushes to round up the ponies.

The quiet island explodes with the shouts of the men.

They crack long whips in the air.

The sounds scare the ponies from their hiding places.

The men drive the ponies to the water's edge.
Then the ponies swim across to Chincoteague.
They strain to keep their heads above the water.
In a few minutes they reach Chincoteague.
They splash ashore and shake the water
from their shiny coats. Then the men drive the ponies
into a large corral or pen. Many thousands of people
visit Chincoteague to watch this exciting roundup.

The stallions fight in the corral.
They attack with their sharp teeth.
They thrash and kick
with their strong legs.
The corral rings with the noise
of their angry squeals and whinnies.
On Assateague the herds can live
far apart. But in the corral
the ponies are crowded together.
Stallions will often fight
when they are so close to each other.

The main reason for the Pony Penning
is to sell many of the new foals.
If all the foals stayed with their herds,
there would not be enough grass
for them to eat.
It is sad to hear the mares
and foals whinny for each other.
But the foals will not be sad for long.
A happy child waits to love each one of them.
Not all the foals are sold.
Each year a few go back to Assateague
and grow up with their herds.

At last the ponies swim back to Assateague.

One muddy mare looks back for a moment.

She may be looking for her foal.

One foal and her mother are still together.

They nuzzle each other as they eat.

The little foal seems very glad

to be back with her family.

The ponies of Assateague have come home again.

At the Pony Penning
the National Geographic Society bought two foals.
They will roam free on the island
for as long as they live. These foals belong
to all children who enjoy
learning about ponies in the wild.

Published by The National Geographic Society
Melvin M. Payne, *President;* Melville Bell Grosvenor, *Editor-in-Chief;*
Gilbert M. Grosvenor, *Editor*

Prepared by
The Special Publications Division
Robert L. Breeden, *Editor*
Donald J. Crump, *Associate Editor*
Philip B. Silcott, *Senior Editor*
Cynthia Russ Ramsay, *Managing Editor*
Elizabeth W. Fisher, *Research*

Design and Art Direction
Joseph A. Taney, *Staff Art Director*
Ursula Perrin, *Assistant Art Director*

Production and Printing
Robert W. Messer, *Production Manager*
George V. White, *Assistant Production Manager*
Raja D. Murshed, June L. Graham, *Production Assistants*
John R. Metcalfe, *Engraving and Printing*
Mary G. Burns, Jane H. Buxton, Stephanie S. Cooke, Natalie
    Iglitz, Suzanne J. Jacobson, Marilyn L. Wilbur, *Staff Assistants*

Consultants
Dr. Glenn O. Blough, *Educational Consultant*
Dr. Henry W. Setzer, *Curator, Division of Mammals,*
    Smithsonian Institution, Washington, D. C.; Scientific Consultant
Edith K. Chasnov, *Reading Specialist*

Donna K. Grosvenor, who wrote this book,
and James L. Stanfield, who took the pictures,
followed the wild ponies for months.
Both grew to know the little ponies well
and gave them names.

PEEKABOO

BIG RED

SUNDANCE